THE GOLD EDITION OF THE
ESSENTIAL PIANO COLLECTION

Published by:
Chester Music Limited,
8/9 Frith Street, London W1D 3JB, England.

Exclusive Distributors:
Music Sales Limited,
Distribution Centre, Newmarket Road, Bury St Edmunds, Suffolk IP33 3YB, England.
Music Sales Corporation,
257 Park Avenue South, New York, NY 10010, United States of America.
Music Sales Pty Limited,
120 Rothschild Avenue, Rosebery, NSW 2018, Australia.

Order No. CH69245
ISBN 1-84449-779-8
This book © Copyright 2005 by Chester Music.

D1546741

Compiled by Michael Ahmad and Heather Ramage.
Music engraved by Note-orious Productions Limited.

Printed in the United States of America by
Vicks Lithograph and Printing Corporation.

Your Guarantee of Quality:
As publishers, we strive to produce every book to the highest commercial standards.
The music has been freshly engraved and carefully designed to minimize
awkward page turns to make playing from it a real pleasure.
Particular care has been given to specifying acid-free, neutral-sized
paper made from pulps which have not been elemental chlorine bleached.
This pulp is from farmed sustainable forests and was produced
with special regard for the environment.
Throughout, the printing and binding have been planned to ensure a sturdy,
attractive publication which should give years of enjoyment.
If your copy fails to meet our high standards, please inform us and we will gladly replace it.

www.musicsales.com

CHESTER MUSIC
part of the Music Sales Group

London/New York/Paris/Sydney/Copenhagen/Berlin/Madrid/Tokyo

Air On The G String

Composed by Johann Sebastian Bach

Concerto No.5 in F Minor

(2nd Movement: Adagio)

Composed by Johann Sebastian Bach

Arranged by Jerry Lanning

In Tears of Grief
(from St. Matthew Passion)

Composed by Johann Sebastian Bach

Arranged by Jerry Lanning

Prelude No.1 in C Major

(from The Well-Tempered Clavier Book I)

Composed by Johann Sebastian Bach

Bagatelle in G Minor, Op.119, No.1

Composed by Ludwig van Beethoven

Allegretto

Sonata Pathétique, Op.13

(2nd Movement: Adagio cantabile)

Composed by Ludwig van Beethoven

Symphony No.5, Op.67

(1st Movement: Allegro con brio)

Composed by Ludwig van Beethoven

Arranged by Jack Long

Allegro con brio (♩ = 108)

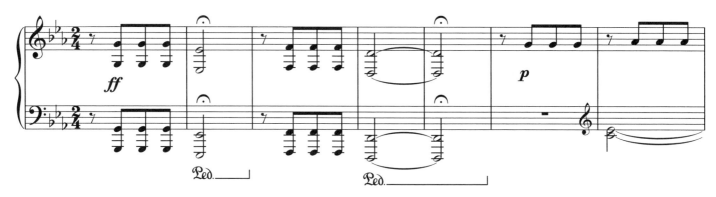

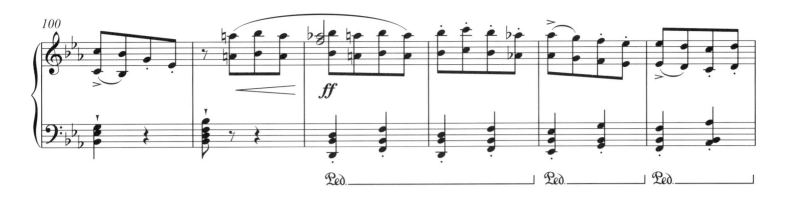

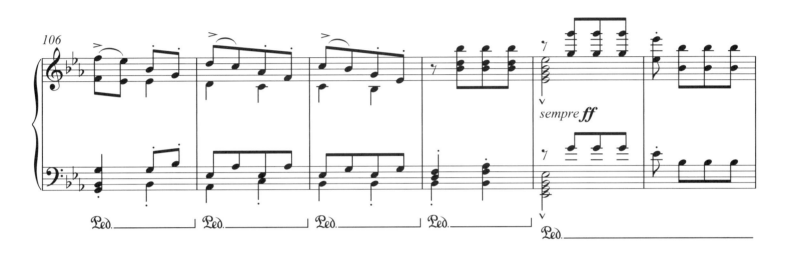

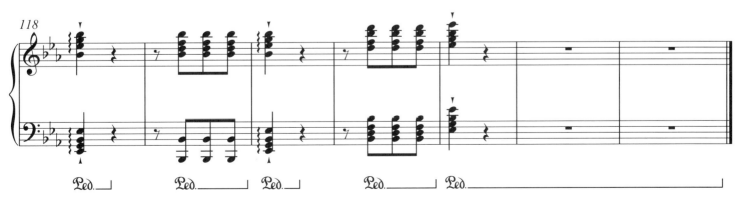

Hungarian Dance in G Minor

Composed by Johannes Brahms

Arranged by Quentin Thomas

Violin Sonata, Op.106, No.3

(2nd Movement: Adagio)

Composed by Johannes Brahms
Arranged by Quentin Thomas

28

Nocturne in E♭, Op.9, No.2

Composed by Frédéric Chopin

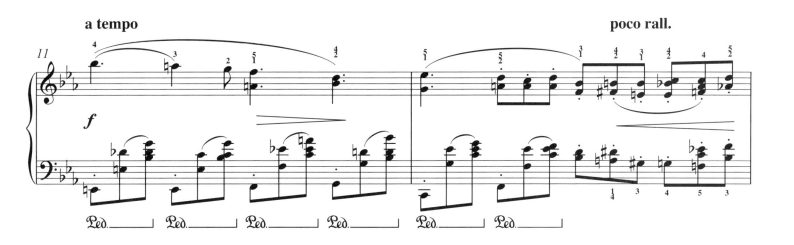

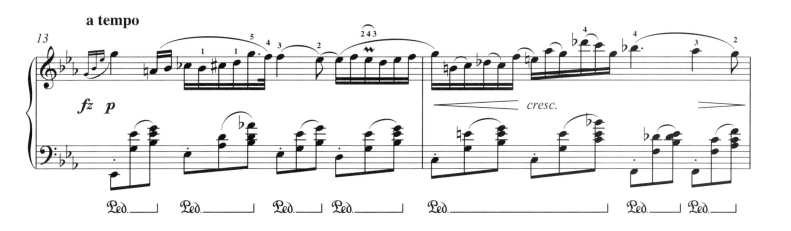

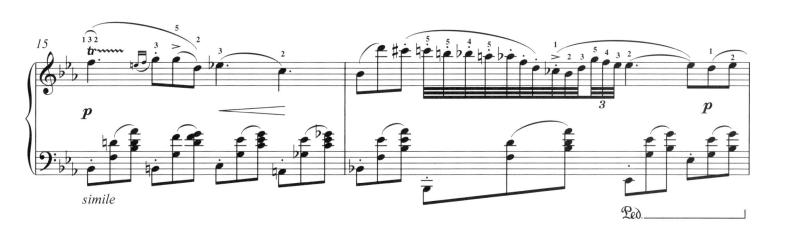

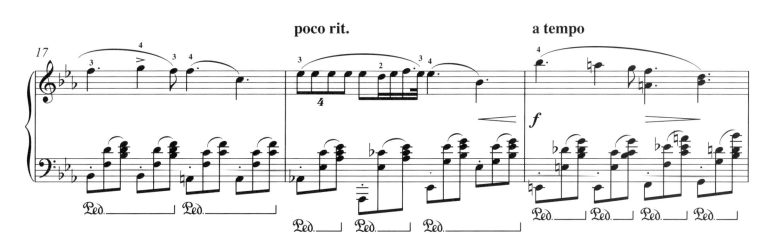

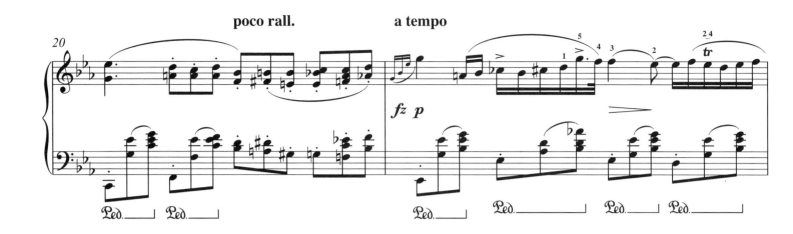

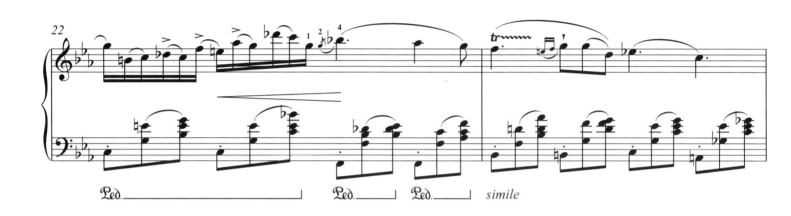

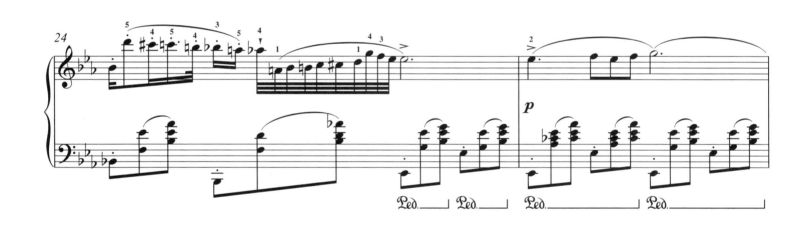

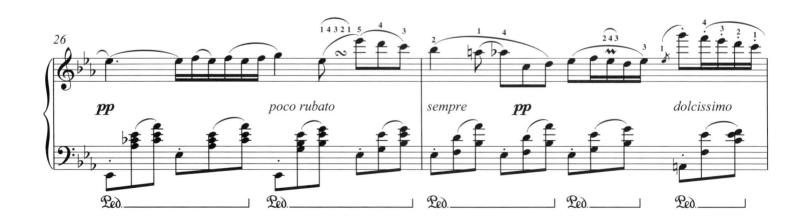

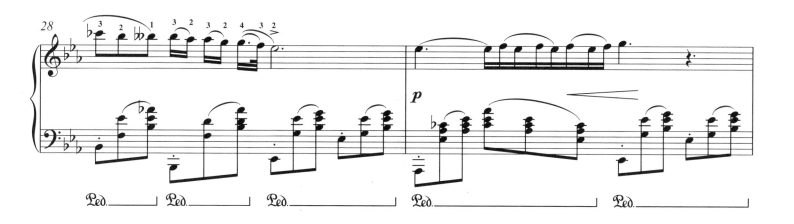

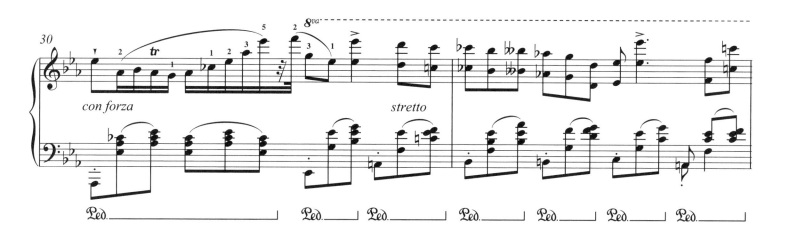

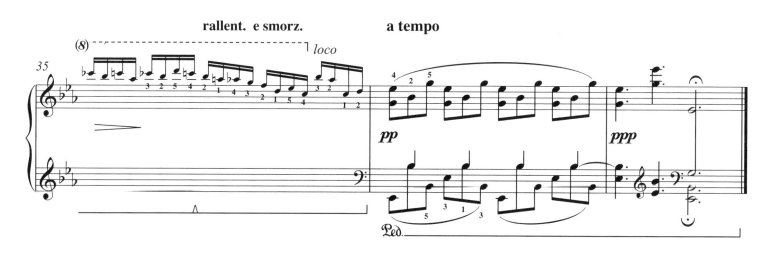

Prelude in E Minor

Composed by Frédéric Chopin

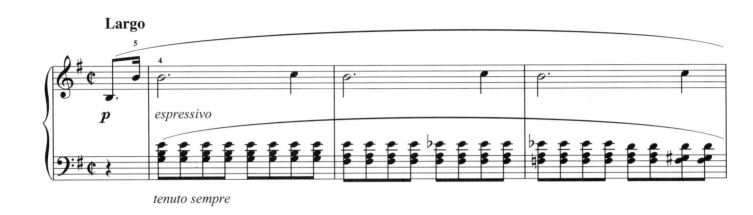

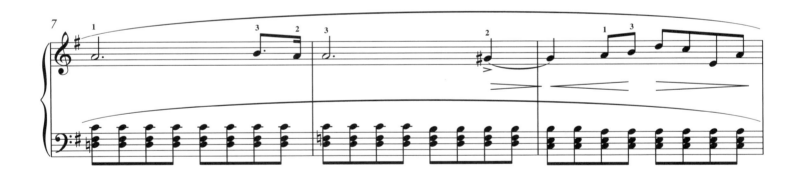

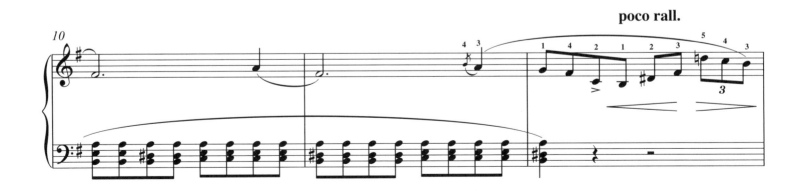

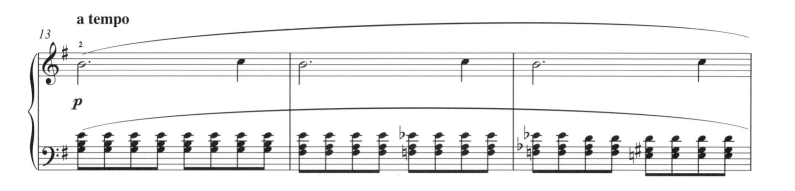

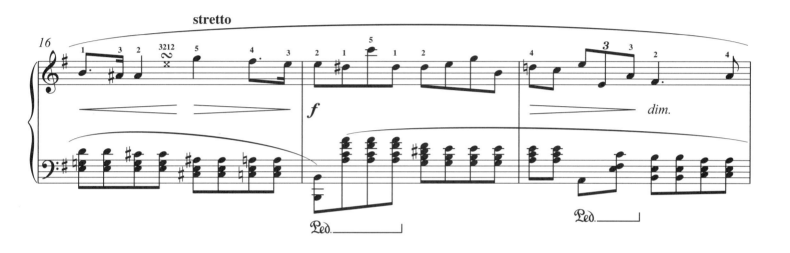

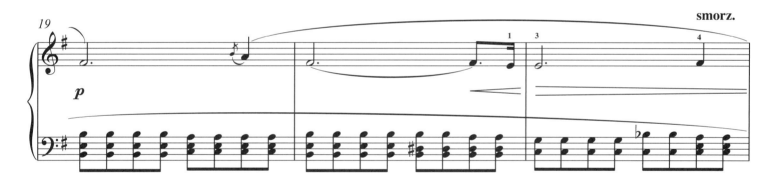

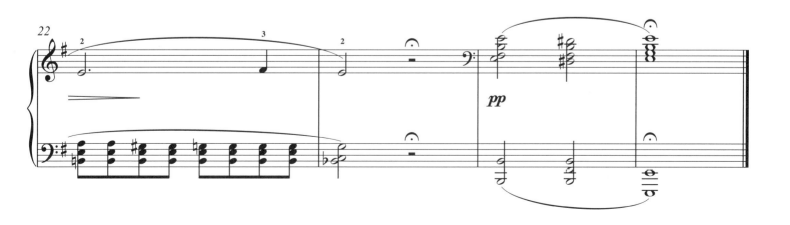

Prelude in C Minor, Op.28

Composed by Frédéric Chopin

The Entertainer

Composed by Scott Joplin

(repeat R.H. 8va higher)

Maple Leaf Rag

Composed by Scott Joplin

Tempo di marcia

Trio

Clair De Lune

Composed by Claude Debussy

Andante très expressif

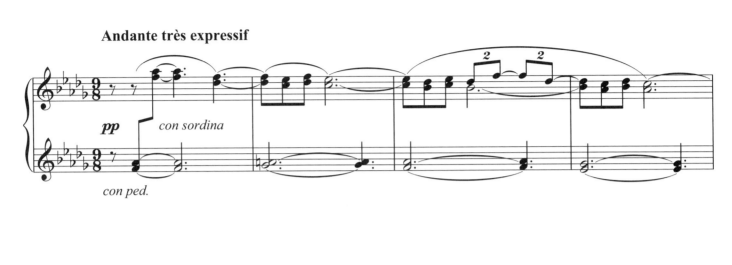

Tempo rubato

Tempo I

pp *morendo jusqu'à la fin*

The Little Shepherd
(from Children's Corner)

Composed by Claude Debussy

Après Un Rêve

Composed by Gabriel Fauré

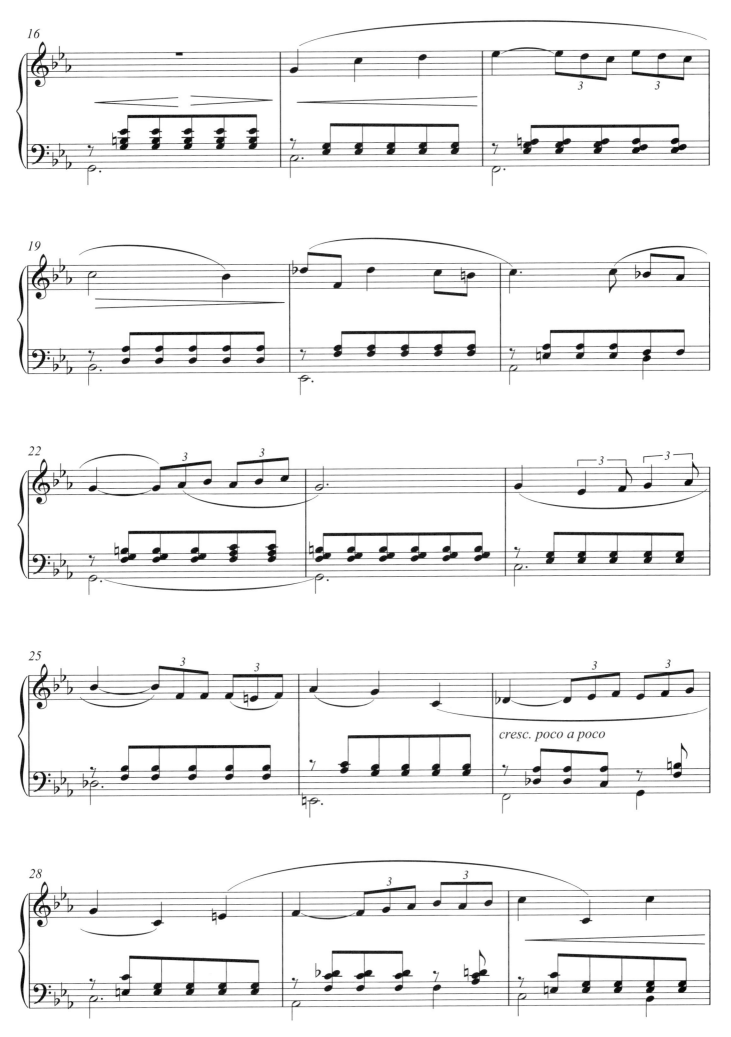

Pavane

Composed by Gabriel Fauré

Andante molto moderato

Air
(from Water Music)

Composed by George Frideric Handel

Zadok The Priest

Composed by George Frideric Handel

Andante maestoso

pp _crescendo poco a poco_

Con ped.

simile

9

mp *sempre cresc.*

11

13

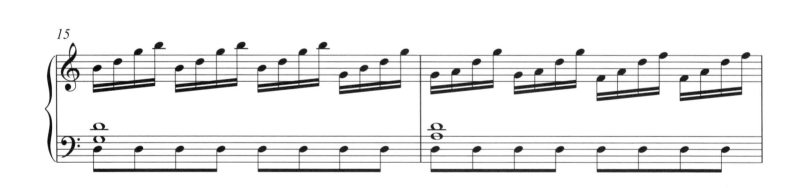

15

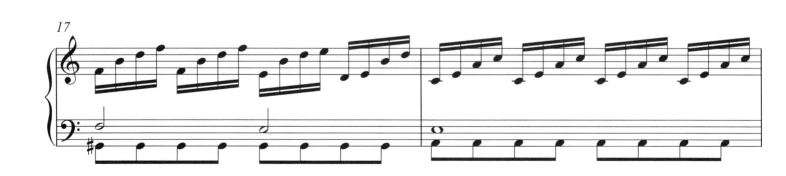

17

Sarabande

Composed by George Frideric Handel

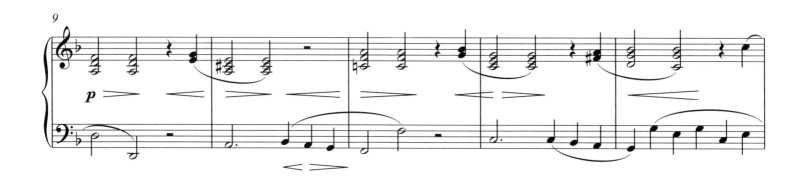

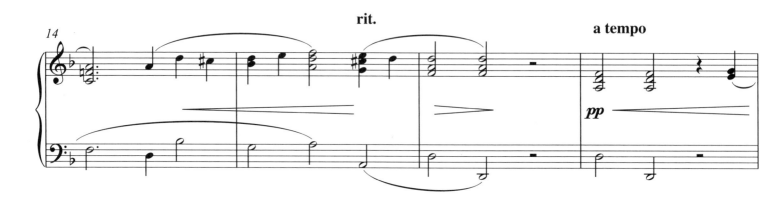

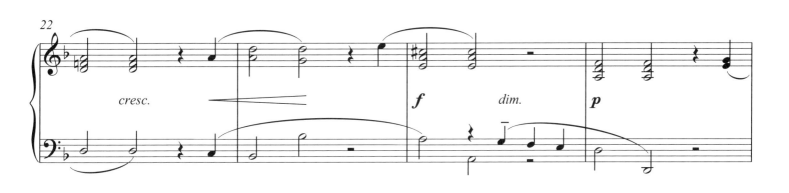

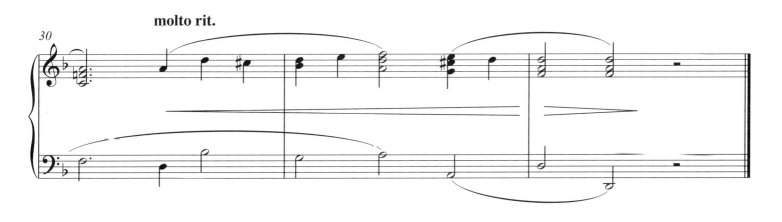

Suite No.7
(3rd Movement: Allegro)

Composed by George Frideric Handel

Fingal's Cave Overture 'Hebrides'

Composed by Felix Mendlessohn

Arranged by Quentin Thomas

Allegro moderato

Sweet Remembrance
(from Songs Without Words, Op.19, No.1)

Composed by Felix Mendlessohn

Arranged by Quentin Thomas

Ave Maria

Composed by Franz Schubert
Arranged by Quentin Thomas

Gute Nacht
(from Winterreise)

Composed by Franz Schubert

Arranged by Quentin Thomas

Träumerei

(from Scenes From Childhood, Op.15, No.7)

Composed by Robert Schumann

Piano Quartet
(3rd Movement: Andante cantabile)

Composed by Robert Schumann

Arranged by Quentin Thomas

cantabile e poco a poco cresc.

rit.

p

March Of The Toys
(from The Nutcracker)

Composed by Pyotr Ilyich Tchiakovsky
Arranged by Barry Todd

Tempo di marcia

Symphony No.5
(2nd Movement: Andante)

Composed by Pyotr Ilyich Tchaikovsky
Arranged by Barry Todd

Andante cantabile

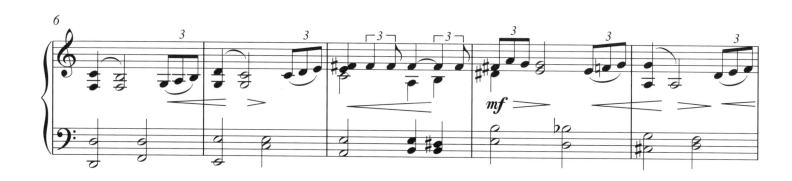

Lacrymosa
(from Requiem)

Composed by Wolfgang Amadeus Mozart

Serenade in B♭ 'Gran Partita'
(3rd Movement: Adagio)

Composed by Wolfgang Amadeus Mozart

Arranged by Jack Long

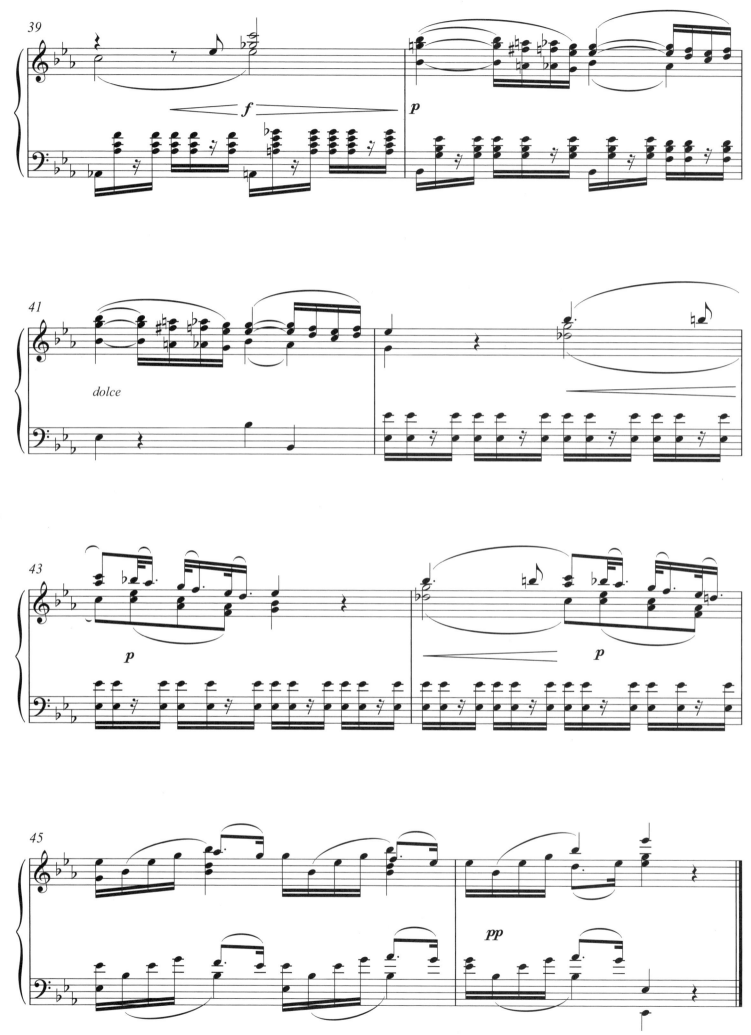